Dear Novice Entrepreneur,

I imagine, since you bought this book, you are seriously considering starting your own business or are in the early phases of a business. What a thrill! What a challenge! What excitement! How scary. How lonely. You will never be the same again.

There are many informative books to help you get started on your road to entrepreneurship. I know because I read many of them. Books on how to write a business plan, finance the business, market your product, sell prospective customers, handle the legal aspects of a business and much more. All this advice is important and I encourage you to find materials on these topics. In fact, to help you get started, I included a list in the back of this book.

As important, however, is your mental attitude—your desire to succeed, your level of commitment, and your unshakable belief in yourself and your dream. Those are the characteristics my guide addresses. Those traits are just as important as getting financing and setting up bookkeeping because they will help get you through the tough times. It is those characteristics that will help you when business is in a slump, you feel like giving up, you feel helpless or hopeless, and you can't sleep because you're afraid to take risks or worried about whether or not you made the right decision.

I hope you will practice these tactics, refer to them often, and share them with fellow entrepreneurs.

Best of luck!
Joan Burge

"The entrepreneur is essentially a visualizer. . .He can visualize something, and when he visualizes it, he sees exactly how to make it happen."

Robert L. Schwartz
The Best of Success

A
SURVIVAL
GUIDE
FOR THE
NOVICE
ENTREPRENEUR

JOAN M. BURGE

Joan Burge
5/98

HAMPTONROADS
PUBLISHING COMPANY, INC.

Hampton Roads Publishing Company, Inc.
891 Norfolk Square
Norfolk, VA 23502
Or call: (804)459-2453
FAX: (804)455-8907

If you are unable to order this book from
your local bookseller, you may order
directly from the publisher.
Call 1-800-766-8009, toll-free.

Cover design by Patrick Smith

ISBN 1-878901-74-5

10 9 8 7 6 5 4 3 2 1

Printed on acid-free paper
in the United States of America

Acknowledgements

I want to acknowledge my husband Dave and my children, Lauren and Brian, for supporting me in my crazy life as an entrepreneur.

A special thanks to the people at Celebrating Excellence, Incorporated, for allowing me to use several quotes from one of their books entitled *The Best of Success*. Their address is listed in the reference section of this book.

Contents

Believe in You

How strong is your belief in *you?* In your vision? In your talents and abilities? Do you believe you have a great idea or talent? Or do you make great decisions only to fill yourself with doubt when someone tells you you're wrong or that your idea will never work?

As an entrepreneur, your belief system has to be literally unshakable. I'm not saying you're never going to be wrong; some of your ideas won't pan out and sometimes you won't make the best decision. What I am saying is that if there is something you truly believe in—an idea, something you want to create, a service you can provide, a way of helping people—then you must keep that belief strong and *go* for it.

I'd like to tell you a little story about how to train a flea. What does that have to do with believing in yourself? Well, read on and I'm sure you'll get the connection.

To train a flea, we need a glass jar with a lid and, obviously, a flea. Before we train our flea, we're going to just put him in the jar without the lid on it. Now what do you think will happen to this flea? What is the flea's main mode of transportation? Of getting around? Jumping, right? So if we don't put the lid on the jar, our flea is probably going to jump out.

Now we want to train our flea. So let's put the lid on the jar. What's going to happen? The flea will jump up several times only to hit the lid. Eventually the flea will learn that if he continues to jump so high, he will hit the lid. Since we have a smart flea, our flea is not going to jump as high anymore. Instead, our flea now will jump only halfway up the jar. What have we done to this flea? We have *conditioned* him. What do you think will happen, now, if we take the lid off the jar? In other words, how high do you think this flea will jump when we take the lid off? If you said halfway, you're right. We have *conditioned* the flea to *believe* he can't jump any higher than halfway. He will not jump out of the jar because he has been conditioned not to.

We are very much the same. We have goals and visions of what we'd like to do. But, from the time we are children and on through our adulthood, most of us are told we can't do certain things. We can't reach our goals. We can't try new things. Our ideas are silly. We therefore condition ourselves to believe we can do no more than what we are doing today—that we have no more potential than what we are today.

There are plenty of people who will question what you are doing and say things to disempower you. Add to those discouraging comments some of your own natural self-doubt and fears, and you're setting yourself up for defeat. Take the lid off your jar and don't let anyone ever put a lid on you again. If you don't have a strong belief in yourself and your dream and faith in the Lord above, chances are you won't succeed over the long term.

Tactics:

1. Believe in you.

2. Learn to trust your judgment—to trust the knowledge you have of yourself.

3. Remember that only you know if you can really do this, really take on a difficult project, really learn that new skill or start that new business.

4. Visually see your belief system as a solid pillar. A pillar that no one can tear down or knock down.

5. Keep a list of empowering quotes in places where you can easily see them.

6. Have faith and pray for guidance, courage, and persistence.

7. Do something that gives you a sense of achievement because that feeling will be to your soul what a vitamin is to your body. (See Chapter on Cycle of Achievement.)

8. Allow your belief in yourself to have flexibility and to grow. Believing in yourself is understanding that you may end up on a different path, because of what you do and what you learn as you go along, than the path

on which your beliefs originally led you.

9. Be aware of negatives being sent out from others. Constantly people throw out negative comments without us truly being aware that we are receiving them. They can get into your subconscious and color your actions and responses.

10. Gravitate to positive, upbeat people. Be with people who encourage and support you, not people who tear you down or make fun of your ideas.

11. Feed your mind with positive self-talk, read positive materials, and listen to inspiring audio tapes.

12. Remember the story about training a flea. Don't let anyone condition you for failure; rather, condition yourself for success.

We can do only what we think we can do. We can be only what we think we can be. We can have only what we think we can have. What we do, what we are, what we have, all depend upon what we think.

Robert Collier

Facing Fear

F-E-A-R: False Evidence Appearing Real. We all have experienced it. Fear comes in different sizes and shapes, has different faces, and, for each of us, is unique. What I fear, you might laugh at and vice versa.

Fear is very real and comes with the territory of first starting a business. The big difference between people is that for some fear paralyzes and for others fear becomes a personal challenge. It gets their adrenalin flowing. Depending on the circumstance and your past experiences in dealing with the emotion, fear can be either one for you—paralyzing or challenging.

Every time you do what you fear and thereby tackle that fear, you become a stronger person. You prepare yourself for bigger and greater things to come. I'm not saying that once you conquer a fear you will never have fear again. It's just that when you learn to deal with a fear and experience some success in taking it on, you will be more inclined to take on the next challenge which might be fearful to you.

I still get scared about my business and certain challenges. I still have fears. I hope to always have them. It means I haven't yet done all I'm capable of doing. I haven't stretched in a new area, taken on a bigger challenge, and mustered up everything I am capable of doing here on earth. I take my fears on as personal challenges. I try very hard not to let a fear paralyze me and cause me to do nothing. And so far, that thinking has worked for me. In less than three years, I have taken on and accomplished things I never imagined. And so I hope it is with you.

Tactics:

1. Remember that the fear of doing something—the thought of doing something that scares you—is many times more difficult to handle than the actual experience. Think back to something you were afraid to do and then actually did it. Chances are that, after you did it, you thought to yourself, "This really wasn't as bad as I imagined."

2. Refuse to dwell on your fear. Be aware that fear can become a monster if you give it room to grow; it becomes bigger in your mind than it really is. Many times we blow up the fear out of proportion and then it overwhelms us.

3. When dealing with the fear of starting a business, making major adjustments to your business, or trying something new in your business, try these steps:
    a. Think through the fear and try to figure out what you are really afraid of. Are you afraid of failure?

Afraid you really don't know what you're doing? Afraid you don't have the manpower to handle the project if it is a success? Afraid you might lose money on the deal? What are you *really* afraid of?

b. Anticipate the worst possible outcome if you do what you fear; decide what you will do should that occur and whether you can live with that situation.

c. Look for all the good things that could happen if you take on the challenge.

d. Take a deep breath and go for it.

4. Be supportive of other people and understand that their fears are very real to them. Help them work through their fears using the steps in Tactic #3.

Courage is a special kind of knowledge; the knowledge of how to fear what ought to be feared, and how to not fear what ought not to be feared. From this knowledge comes the inner strength that subconsciously inspires us to push on in the face of great difficulty. What can seem impossible is often possible, with courage.

Best of Success

Write a Business Plan

Before you open your doors or hang out that sign or hire one employee, do yourself a big favor and write your business plan.

I'm not going to tell you how to write one. There are several good books and resources to guide you. (See references in the back of the book.) But I will tell you how important it is to your success and to keeping yourself on track.

I might have been a novice entrepreneur when I officially opened my business full-time on September 1, 1990, but I knew a business plan was a necessity long before then. Maybe it's because I worked in the business world, mostly corporate, for twenty years before starting my own business and I knew the importance of planning.

I didn't specifically know how to write a plan or all of the pieces that were supposed to go in it, but I knew it was the most logical thing to do before officially opening a business. To help me get started, I wrote to the Small Business Administration in our area and requested information, after which I made a personal visit for counseling. The SBA offers many free services of which you should take advantage early on. I also bought some books to guide me along and received some outlines from other entrepreneurs while attending seminars on how to start a small business.

Tactics:

1. Discipline yourself to write a plan before you open your doors.

2. Discipline yourself to adjust and update your plan once a year, preferably two to three months prior to the beginning of your fiscal year.

3. Get outlines and directions on what should be in a plan from the SBA and SCORE; they specialize in writing plans and can provide you with materials and books.

4. You may want to present a slightly different plan when applying for a loan than what you have written for your own information. I learned this tip from a financial planner when I was getting ready to apply for a loan. This financial planner told me that a bank is interested in the bottom line—the numbers and my ability to pay back the loan. They weren't necessarily interested in all the bells and whistles of the business.

5. If necessary, have your accountant help you with the financial section of your plan. I'm not very numbers-oriented and yet the numbers are very important in running a business. I can

manage the basics of bookkeeping and keeping records for my business but have easy access to my accountant when I need help or advice; and, of course, my accountant handles any financial projects or reports.

6. If necessary, get assistance from a financial planner. Once I had my business plan in a close-to-finished format, I had a financial advisor fine-tune it. He saw things I didn't. He critiqued my entire plan and made some excellent recommendations.

There are those who travel and those who are going somewhere. They are different and yet they are the same. The success has this over his rivals: he knows where he is going.

Mark Caine
Best of Success

Have a Fallback Plan

I always knew that if my business were to fail—if my idea were to be unsuccessful—I had three alternatives to fall back upon. This is important. Before you officially start your business, you should know exactly what you will do if your idea doesn't work. It's like having a parachute when you free-fall from a plane; you should always have an extra chute should your first parachute fail.

Having a fallback plan gives you that little bit of comfort that comes from knowing what you will do should your idea not fulfill your expectations. I really don't believe in the word *fail*, however. If you at least tried something, then you are a success and certainly ahead of the person who will never try anything. Yes, you might have more to lose, but you also have gained in the process.

Many times, people interpret the failure of an idea to be a reason to give up. That's not necessarily true. Maybe just that particular idea didn't work. Maybe it needed to be approached from a different angle. My business, a consulting and training business, is not an easy business to start and maintain. I have to consistently seek out new clients while keeping up with the old and working on the present. There are periods when I have had days of bad news—even weeks of everything going wrong. But I don't see those times as failures. I see them as a challenge to work harder and smarter.

So sometimes failure is a mirage. It appears to be real but it really isn't failure. Make sure your failures aren't mirages. But have a fallback plan ready to implement when it's necessary to acknowledge that your idea isn't working out.

Tactics:

1. Have at least one fallback plan. Two to three would even be better. Plan them early on so you know exactly what you would do should your idea for your new business not take off as you expect. This will give you a certain level of comfort which comes from being prepared.

2. Occasionally re-evaluate your fallback plan. Although your business might be doing well, it's possible that economic times will change, the market place will change, or a competitor will knock you out of the box.

3. Don't get so comfortable in your success that you are blinded by something that could drastically affect your business.

Remember you will not always win. Some days, the most resourceful will taste defeat. But there is, in this case, always tomorrow— after you have done your best to achieve success today.

Maxwell Maltz
Best of Success

Don't Keep Your Plan a Secret

Let your children, family and friends know your plans. Share with them your vision for yourself, for your company growth, and for all of you. The life of an entrepreneur is not easy and definitely changes your life style. You might work all day during the week plus put in evenings and occasional weekends. Your work schedule impacts your family and you should be aware of the impact it has. It impacts every part of your life.

Many spouses are afraid for many reasons when their partners decide to go on their own, to have their own businesses. To be their own bosses. I get tremendous support from my husband, but it hasn't been easy on him. It's not easy for my children, either, having a mother who has a crazy schedule. But from the start, I told them many times over why it was important for me to do this and how we would all reap the benefits as a family, and I asked for their support.

Entrepreneurs can get very wrapped up in their work because they usually are doing what they love. But entrepreneurs must never forget the ones who love them and still need them as a father, mother, friend, daughter, or son.

Tactics:

1. Once you know your plan for starting your business, share it with others in your house and with people who are near to you.

2. Let these people know ahead of time that sometimes you might seem a bit out of sorts, more irritable than usual, and tell them why. Starting a business isn't easy; you will have some anxiety, stress, and frustration which you may unintentionally take out on others once in awhile.

3. Ask for their forgiveness in advance and for their help. Also reassure them that the rewards will come eventually as a result of hard labors now. When you start your business, your family might have to make certain sacrifices. So you want to consistently reassure them that their sacrifices and yours will pay off. And it will, if you just wait long enough and give yourself and your business a chance.

4. As you progress, keep your family abreast of what you are doing. If you learn to share your dreams and let others know what you are doing, and they see your accomplishments, they will get excited with you.

5. If your spouse and/or family isn't excited about what you are doing, that is O.K., too. No one will *ever* be as excited about what you are doing as you. You are giving birth to an idea, a vision. It is yours and no one can experience and feel the exhilaration for what you are doing as much as you.

6. Be considerate and non-aggressive about your plan and enthusiasm with others. Sometimes it takes time for people to come around.

It is possible to give away and become richer! It is also possible to hold on too tightly and lose everything. Yes, the liberal man shall be rich! By watering others, he waters himself.

Proverbs 24:25

Sleepless Nights

I remember clearly the first several months when I started my business. The Gulf War had just broken out. The country was in a deep recession. I had just moved to a new city. This was not a good time to start a business, especially a training and consulting business, because often, when times are tough, the first thing companies cut out of their budget is funds for training. So why did I start my business at this time? Go back in time with me for a moment to 1988.

I was working a full-time job in North Carolina for a division of a major corporation. By this time, I had worked as an executive secretary, as a marketing assistant, and in positions with other similar titles for eighteen years. I had worked for twelve different companies during that time while living in five different states; I had worked for businesses ranging from small companies to Fortune 500 companies.

I was getting burned out. I wanted to make a change, but I wasn't sure what kind of change. I was in my mid-thirties, and all I knew was that I didn't want to be still sitting behind a desk working for someone else when I was forty.

I started to share some of this frustration and soul-searching with a good friend of mine named Vo. It was Vo who suggested that I go into consulting and training. Very quickly, our conversations led us from one thing to another and soon to the creation of Office Dynamics.

Vo and I planned to jointly consult and conduct workshops. We were not, however, in a position to quit our full-time jobs; so we started doing some seminars outside of work and I began doing some training for employees where I worked.

Six months later my husband received a job promotion which moved us to Memphis, Tennessee. Office Dynamics was split and somewhat forgotten. I moved away thinking I couldn't do it on my own. My husband and I bought a new home in Memphis, and I took a job as a mortgage lender—something I had never done but was quickly trained to do. I hated it and, after three months, went to work for Coppertone in Memphis. But I was never really happy, and the concept of Office Dynamics kept creeping into my mind. Before I knew it, I decided to do it on my own and proceeded to learn about starting a small business; I learned how to be a trainer, practiced speaking, and wrote an article that was published in a trade magazine.

Coppertone then went through some re-organization in management and my position was targeted to be phased out. I accepted a job with a bank, where I conducted some training. All this time, I was itching to do my business full-time but was too scared to give up a regular paycheck and some of that job security. Six months later, my husband's company was put up for sale, he was recruited by a company in Virginia Beach, and we moved there.

It was at this point (now almost two years since the inception of Office Dynamics) that my husband said to me, "You have to make a choice.

You have to either give up Office Dynamics or go full-time because you're making yourself (and the family) crazy."

There was no way I would give up the concept of Office Dynamics, and I knew my husband was right. I knew the only way I would know whether my idea would work was to devote 100 percent of my time to it. Little did I know, however, that soon after my decision the Gulf war would break out and circumstances would change—which now brings us to the start of my business full-time.

Being new in that part of the country, I didn't know a soul. I didn't even know how to get to downtown. I spent the first three months writing training programs and participant workbooks and finding out who was who in town. I spent the next two months introducing myself and making personal visits to businesses in the area. Every day I'd call my answering service to see if there were messages from potential clients. I would hear the same response over and over. "You're all clear—no messages." That was not exactly what I wanted to hear. Obviously, during those first six months I didn't get much sleep. Actually, I didn't book my first seminar until after eight months. I waited eight months for my first paycheck!

At one point, I was so nervous about getting the business going that my face broke out. Real nice for someone who has to be in the public eye and speak in front of groups of people! What kept me going? What kept me from just throwing in the towel and going to work for someone else? Persistence. Patience. Faith. And belief in my work. Belief that someday I would have lots of phone messages! Eventually I began getting scheduled to conduct workshops and guest speaking. And yes, my face finally cleared up and I finally slept at night.

Oh, there are times I have sleepless nights, like right now, as I write this chapter at 3:00 a.m. But now my sleepless nights come more from excitement and enthusiasm. And yes, even from being faced with major challenges; but I have learned to deal with the challenges.

Tactics:

1. Be prepared for sleepless nights. Sleepless nights worrying whether your idea will be successful, sleepless nights worrying about finances, sleepless nights worrying about all the work you have to do.

2. If you are married, prepare your spouse for disruptive nights and decide together how you'll handle them. Will you lie in bed tossing and turning, telling yourself "go to sleep" or will you wake your partner up and talk about what's bothering you or will you turn on a night light and read?

3. Get up and do something constructive. That's one fortunate (and sometimes unfortunate) thing about having your office in your home or bringing work home with you. Instead of lying in bed, get up and do something. Work

on an idea. Work on a solution to what you are worrying about. Work on something that doesn't take any brain power or read from the stack of "to read" pile you have accumulated. Eventually you'll get tired and go back to sleep. You may even feel like you've taken a load off your mind. You may go to bed feeling really good because you've come up with an answer to your problem.

Commit yourself to a dream. . . Nobody who tries to do something great but fails is a total failure. Why? Because he can always rest assured that he succeeded in life's most important battle—he defeated the fear of trying.

Robert H. Schuller

Never, Never Give Up

Where would we be if Edison had given up? If the Wright Brothers had given up? If all the inventors and creators of ideas and products had given up? I don't know, but I'm glad they all persisted. Persistence is a great strength for anyone in any walk of life; it is one of utmost importance to an entrepreneur.

As an entrepreneur you are going to experience setbacks, face hardships, and come up against brick walls. Sometimes just as you think you have recovered from a setback and things are turning around for the better, something will happen to change everything. Often you will have a decision to make—quit or persist. I encourage you to persist. If you give up, you'll never know how things might have turned out for you.

If you were to read my personal diary since the day I started my business, you would read that in the first twelve months I was tempted to quit several times. But every time I had that thought, that's all it was; I did not translate that thought into action. I am so thankful today that I didn't give up on my dreams. As hard as the road as been and still is because of new challenges, I have been rewarded in many ways. Had I given up when I felt most discouraged, I wouldn't have had all the wonderful experiences that I have had and continue to have; I wouldn't have met the many wonderful people whom I've met; and I wouldn't be able to write this book, which hopefully will help you.

Tactics:

1. When things aren't working out as you expected, make adjustments or take a different route. You don't necessarily have to scratch your entire idea or project. It might just need some fine-tuning.

2. Hang tough—ride the waves. Don't wimp out when the going gets tough. That is when the real challenge begins. It's easy to hang in there when things are going your way, but can you hang tough when things are falling apart and money isn't coming in and customers aren't calling? What are you going to do? Wimp out or hang tough?

3. *Persistence.* Remember this word. Plant it right now in your brain. Every time you feel discouraged or feel like you want to quit, see that word in your mind—*persistence.* Say the word to yourself. Say it out loud. Say "I will persist in the face of adversity."

4. Think to yourself "What if tomorrow I win? What if tomorrow I make that breakthrough?" You have no idea what tomorrow might bring and you won't know if you give up today.

5. Realize that there will be setbacks. In fact, count on it. But also tell yourself that you won't pick up your marbles and run away. Tell yourself that you can survive, and eventually you will thrive.

6. Think of all the wonderful things you enjoy, use in your life, and take for granted. Would you have those "things" if someone had not persisted?

The power to hold on in spite of every-thing, the power to endure—this is the winner's quality. *Persistence* is the ability to face defeat again and again without giving up—to push on in the face of great difficul-ty, knowing that victory can be yours. *Persistence* means taking pains to overcome every obstacle, and to do what's necessary to reach your goals.

Best of Success

Patience

Patience is a virtue that was difficult for me to acquire in matters concerning my business. I'm the kind of person who wants something *now*. When I have a vision, I want it to be my reality soon.

I wanted my business to be successful right away. I wanted to write books, do audio and video tapes, and take off like a rocket! Don't get me wrong. I still do, but I have tempered all that energy and excitement with patience; or maybe life forced me to be more patient because it said, "Joan, you must first go through this before you can get to that."

At first, I didn't understand that there is a process one must go through. I didn't understand that there are certain lessons one must learn before being ready to take something on. There will always be a select few individuals who will start something and become instantly successful. But most of the great successes I have read about and met paid their dues. Paid them in the form of setbacks, financial distress, personal tragedy, or the necessity of scrapping their entire ideas and starting fresh.

Tactics:

1. Practice patience. It's so hard for us to do this in a society that wants everything *now*. A society that says you must have it all by the time you're forty. You must have the big house soon, the fancy car today, the flashy clothes yesterday. Practice patience.

2. Enjoy the process. After all, half the fun is in getting there. (See Enjoy The Process).

3. Keep close at hand some quotes regarding patience so that, when you feel terribly impatient, you can read a reminder to get yourself on track.

4. Read about successful people. About several of them. You will find that it took years of hard work and sometimes heartaches and setbacks before they reached their true destinies.

5. Be patient in achieving success. It will come one piece at a time. Slowly but surely.

History has demonstrated that the most notable winners usually encountered heartbreaking obstacles before they triumphed. They won because they refused to become discouraged by their defeats.

B. C. Forbes

Mirror Mirror

How do you see yourself? Do you see yourself as bright, energetic, professional, and self-confident? Do you see yourself as someone who is responsible for his success as well as failure? Or do you see yourself as scared, not too sure of what you're doing and not an expert?

What's going on inside you shows on the outside. What do you want to reflect to others? To yourself? Your self-image is so important, especially when first starting a business, because:

1. You don't have a company being written about in *Inc.* magazine yet,

2. You don't have an established track record to tell yourself and others how well you are doing, and

3. You might not have the money to buy the fancy office or store and hire staff that would give a successful impression to customers immediately.

So, you must have a good self-image. How you see yourself will dictate your actions, which are what others see. It also will dictate how you handle certain situations. How you manage certain challenges. How you treat your staff, if you have one. It will send out messages loud and clear to your customers as to what kind of person you are and what kind of business philosophy you have.

Do a check on your self-image. Is it where it should be? Is it where you want it to be? How can it be improved?

Tactics:

1. Think about who you want to be and the image you want to reflect. Then set it in your mind.

2. Practice mental imaging, visualization, and affirmations. There are volumes of materials on these subjects.

3. Remember that if you act as a business professional you will be treated as one and respected.

4. Refuse to let others dictate to you who they think you should be. You set the image of who you want to be.

5. On a sheet of paper, write a list of your strengths and then list areas for growth. Use the qualities under your strengths as much as possible and then work on those traits listed under areas for growth. Your objective should be to eventually move the skills and abilities listed under "areas

for growth" to your "strengths" column and then add new skills and abilities to the "areas for growth" column. As you grow and as your company grows, you will need to develop new skills. I hope you will always have things listed under "areas for growth" because that means you are growing as a person. The quickest avenue to mental and spiritual death is stagnation—believing you have nothing more to learn. I hope you will grow for years to come.

The picture you have of yourself is exactly the way you will perform.

Don't Settle For Anything Less

I will not settle for anything less than:

—Achieving personal excellence;
—Being successful, according to my definition of success;
—Giving my clients the best service possible in my industry;
—Having the best product in my area of expertise.

From the time that I first started my business, it has been unacceptable to me to fail. The thought of going back to work for someone else is inconceivable. Therefore, I had to make it all work. Somehow, some way, I would not give up my dream. A few times when I felt as though I would never make it because I wasn't getting phone calls from clients, I would pull out the Help Wanted section of the paper, skim over it, and say to myself "No way."

Today it is still unacceptable for me to quit, to fail, or to achieve anything other than professional and personal excellence. For what are you going to settle?

Tactics:

1. Set high personal standards. Set standards that will make you grow and stretch. If you set mediocre standards, that's what you will achieve. If you settle for being a mediocre entrepreneur, that is what you will be. If you settle for giving your customers mediocre service, that is what you will give. Don't settle for mediocrity—strive for stardom!

2. Compete only with yourself. Be aware of what your competitors are doing, but then get your focus back to yourself and your business.

3. Recognize what you value. What is the one or two values you hold highest? Are they honesty, integrity, and excellence? These will be driving forces in how you deal with customers, employees, and other business associates.

4. Don't be afraid to set high sales goals. I didn't say totally unrealistic goals; rather, set sales goals that, with hard work and persistence, you could conceivably reach.

5. **Remember that if you settle for anything less, that's exactly what you will get.**

Going far beyond the call of duty, doing more than you expect. . . this is what excellence is all about. And it comes from striving, maintaining the highest standards, looking after the smallest detail, and going the extra mile. Excellence means doing your very best. In everything. In every way.

Best of Success

Commitment→Conduct→Character
A Lesson From a Preacher

November 15, 1992—a very special day in my life—the day I officially accepted Christ into my life. No, the heavens didn't open and God didn't speak to me. But that's an entire story in itself. During the sermon in church that day the preacher talked about commitment leading to conduct leading to character. *Wow!* What a thought.

In addition to the applications of that concept in the spiritual sense, I thought about how that applied in a business sense. That statement defines what can make anyone a success at whatever he sets out to do in life. And it has vital relevance to the entrepreneur.

In other words, if you are truly committed to your work—to your vision, to whatever you set out to do—the conduct will follow. And as you conduct yourself with positive action and attitude, taking little steps every day toward your goals, you will build character. Isn't that wonderful? Such a simple formula and yet so hard for people to do. Think about it.

Tactic:

There's only one real tactic here because, if you use it, the rest will follow.

BE COMMITTED
to yourself and whatever you set out to
do as long as it is right, just, and
doesn't hurt others and remember. . .

**COMMITMENT leads to→CONDUCT leads
to→CHARACTER**

Commandments of Being Committed

★ Thou shalt fear no failure.
★ Thou shalt follow your own path.
★ Thou shalt try and try again.
★ Thou shalt perform to the best of your ability.
★ Thou shalt not just coast along in life, but soar to full potential.
★ Thou shalt not give up.
★ Thou shalt see obstacles only as a test of one's commitment.
★ Thou shalt practice perseverance and patience.
★ Thou shalt set high ideals and have great hope.

Enlist Free Help

As a small business person, even as your company grows, you will always be searching for ways to cut expenses wherever possible. What is most difficult about being a novice entrepreneur is that you usually don't have the ability to hire immediately all the talent you need and/or want. You might be high on ideas and enthusiasm but low on manpower. I was when I first started. In fact, I was a one-man team: sales person, bookkeeper, marketing rep, writer, trainer, speaker, inventory manager, supply orderer, and secretary! It's tough trying to manage all those things when there are just so many hours in a day and so many days in a week.

What I learned about using interns to help me keep up can also benefit you, whether you are a one-person outfit or a fifty-person company. The point is we all want to cut costs, increase productivity, and use our time wisely. Are you asking yourself "What would I do with an intern?" Whether your office is in your home or elsewhere, interns can be of tremendous help on a variety of tasks or projects; an intern can maintain client lists using the computer or some other method, handle routine office tasks such as filing and typing, assemble materials, order supplies, do light bookkeeping, conduct research, assemble your promotional pieces and so forth. The list is endless; let this brief list stimulate your thinking and create your own list of possibilities.

Many times you can find interns who will work for free through local business schools or colleges. I worked with over nine interns during my first two years. They all were assets to me. Usually interns fall into one of three categories: (1) students in their early twenties going to college or attending a business school, (2) mature individuals going to school to prepare for going back to work, or (3) mature individuals preparing to go into the work world for the first time. Interns in any of these categories are energetic, willing and anxious to learn. They want to find out if what they are studying in school fits the "real" work world.

If the interns you use don't get paid, how do they benefit from giving up their time and energy? In several ways:

1. They can use you as a reference when looking for paid employment.

2. They might end up with a paid full-time job from you.

3. They might end up with employment due to your many contacts. You may refer them to someone you know who is hiring.

4. They are learning to apply what they know to the real work world. I have found this to be the greatest payback with the interns I used.

It really can be a win-win situation.

Tactics:

1. Analyze the tasks you perform and determine whether there are any that you could have an intern do.

2. Decide what type of intern you will need to do which tasks or jobs. From that analysis, decide which school you need to approach.

3. Call your local college, business school, secretarial school, or computer school.

4. Ask for the Career Placement Director or Business Department head. If you need an intern to perform editing and proofreading, contact the English Department at a college. If you need an intern to conduct marketing, speak to the Marketing Department head or chairman. If you want an intern to create graphics and add pizzazz to presentation packets, the schools offering computer courses are an excellent source.

5. Be specific. Let the director or department head know:
   a. There will be no payment on your part, if that is the case. Not all interns will work for free. Some will require a minimum fee or want you to at least pay their transporta-

tion. (If you end up of paying anyone, be sure to check with your accountant; some situations—hours worked, etc.—cause an intern to be considered your employee, and then you are responsible for taxes. Whenever in doubt, call your accountant!)

b. What this person will be doing. Will this person be helping you out with administrative duties? Conducting research? Working on the computer? Assisting on a one-time special project?

c. How long you need the intern. As long as he is available? Just through the summer? Just for a particular project?

d. What skills you require and attributes you are looking for. I always stressed that I wanted someone who is dependable.

e. Where the intern will work and how soon you will need him/her.

6. Interview interns. You want to see them and question them as to their abilities and what they hope to gain from the internship. This usually takes no more than a half-hour per intern.

7. Realize that you will have to spend some time training your intern; maybe you have someone else on your staff

who can do this. Be sure to let your interns know when they have done a good job and where they excel. It builds their level of confidence which in turn increases their value to you.

8. Remember that when you use interns you are contributing to the development of other human beings.

Focus on the contribution that you can make.

Peter Drucker

Commitment To Quality

I'm not going to rattle on about TQM (Total Quality Management), Quality Service, Continuous Improvement, or TQL (Total Quality Leadership) in this book. I will just tell you that it is an area you must pursue; choose whatever method appeals to you—read, attend some seminars, hire consultants to teach you and your employees—to learn about this quickly emerging trend. Although the concepts have been around for over twenty years, they are now spreading like wildfire.

Everywhere I turn, I see programs on quality, books on quality, video and audio tapes on quality, and companies investing a lot of money teaching their employees about quality. It's good stuff! But I'm not going to teach it to you. There are some excellent books you can read, some of which I have listed with the references. Just make sure you pick some of them up, read them, take out the critical concepts, and implement them.

Tactics:

1. Set your standards for quality before you open your doors. You need to know what you mean by quality service and products before you can deliver them to your customers.

2. Remember. . .quality does not stop. It is continuous improvement. It is consistently striving to be the best you can be, delivering the best products possible, training your employees to be the best they can be, and constantly meeting customer needs.

3. Commit yourself to being a quality person.

4. Learn the concepts of quality. (See reference list.)

5. Teach the concepts of quality to every person who works for you, not just top management.

6. Realize that every day is an opportunity to be better than yesterday. Every day is an opportunity to manage quality work and quality relationships.

Success in your work, the finding of a better method, the better understanding that insured the better performing is hat and coat, is food and wine, is fire and hose and is health and holiday. At least, I find success in my work has the effect on my spirits of all these.

Ralph Waldo Emerson

Find a Mentor

A *mentor* is defined as "a wise and trusted counselor." My first real mentor was a man for whom I worked more than ten years ago in a large corporation. Since then, I have been fortunate to have other mentors—people I admire, people to whom I can turn and with whom I can talk about my goals. People of whom I can ask questions knowing that they are willing to share the answers. These people have become valuable to me. I am thankful to have had them in my life and know I will always seek out mentors.

Tactics:

1. Find a mentor who:
    a. Is a successful business person;
    b. Works in a similar capacity as you or in your area of interest;
    c. Can teach you the technical aspects of running a business;
    d. Is willing to meet with you a few times a year;
    e. Is not threatened by you.

2. Take this person to lunch. It will be one of the best investments of your time and money.

3. Ask questions. Don't be afraid to ask your mentors lots of questions. Chances are they know they are mentoring and enjoy the role. I remember when I first started my business, I used to meet for lunch with a successful business woman who acted as a mentor to me. When we first began meeting, I always had a list of specific questions I wanted to ask her. After meeting with me a few times, she eventually said to me, "So, where's your list of questions, Joan?" And out they'd come.

4. Give thanks to and show appreciation for your mentor's input.

5. Keep in touch with your mentor on a regular basis. It's always good to stay in touch even when he/she no longer directly mentors you.

6. Ask your mentor for names of the professional people he/she uses, such as attorney, accountant, and banker. You can also ask for your mentor's printer, ad creator, and source of supplies. Such information is valuable, and I recommend you use the people

your mentor uses and recommends. Obviously, your mentor—a successful business person—works with trustworthy vendors and suppliers, people who do good work. Why waste your time, energy, and money hunting through the phone book?

7. In turn, as you grow as an entrepreneur and grow in your field, be a mentor to others. It's a gratifying feeling to help someone who will be having the same fears and questions you now have.

Plans go wrong with too few counselors; many counselors bring success.

Proverbs 15:22

Goal Mapping

Until five years ago, I didn't know what it really meant to set and implement goals. Anthony Robbins gives a perfect example of how most people set goals: they sit down with paper and pencil every New Year's, write down their New Year's resolutions and then never look at them again until the end of the year.

I owe much of my early knowledge about setting goals to Brian Tracy, an international speaker and seminar leader. Five years ago, he was the first person to whom I started to listen regularly via audio and video tapes. I use the term *goal mapping* because planning for your future—both short-term and long-term—can be compared to taking a long road trip. Let's say that I ask you to drive from Virginia Beach, Virginia, to Tuscon, Arizona, without a map. You might get there, but:

—It will take you longer than if you had a
  map,
—You may get lost several times,
—You will waste time,
—You may take some wrong roads, and
—You could get so frustrated that you give
  up and go back to Virginia Beach.

It's the same thing in mapping out your goals. It's not good enough to just write your goals down, although that is an extremely important step and one that is difficult for many people. You must also write out your plan as to how you will reach those goals. What tools do you need? What knowledge? Do you need to involve others? Financial requirements? How long will it take you? You need to set deadlines and specifically identify what obstacles may come your way.

I could write a book about goals but won't because there are plenty of them out there. I suggest you invest in one or several.

I am an absolute believer that you can map out where you want to go. I'm not saying it will be a smooth road that is obstacle-free. But you can learn how to deal with the obstacles. To show you the value of goal mapping, here are a few things I set out to do and accomplished within just thirty months of starting my business:

— Published my first book;
— Started my own professional organization;
— Wrote fourteen full-day training programs and over thirty-five mini-speeches;
— Convinced two major companies to sponsor me at conventions;
— Published my first audio tape program;
— Appeared on local TV and radio and in the newspaper;
— Joined three professional organizations and served on the Board of one of them;
— Obtained national business;
— Wrote my second book (you are reading it);
— Had a client list that included such fine companies and agencies as NASA, Marriott Corporation, Battelle Research Institute, An-

heuser-Busch, Canon of Virginia, Department of the Army, Department of the Navy, Bausch & Lomb, Clemson University.

It is incredible what you can accomplish if you will discipline yourself to write your goals down, determine approximately how long it will take to accomplish them, and write exactly what steps you will have to take to make them happen. Then you must monitor your progress regularly. I have heard many people recommend monitoring your progress monthly. I do a status check about every ten to fifteen days for all major goals.

I have a sheet typed up with each main goal or project listed. I then put those sheets in my follow-up system to pull every ten to fifteen days (or longer if I'm not going to be in town) and then write down my progress. What does this do for me? It. . .

1. Consistently keeps my goals in front of me;

2. Lets me know if I'm falling behind schedule on projects with deadline dates;

3. Lets me know when I'm ahead of schedule (and allows me to feel good about what I'm doing);

4. Permits me to reprioritize or set a different value to a particular goal. (Maybe the goal was an "A" priority goal when I started out, but after a while I realized it was really a "B" or "C." Or maybe a new project came along that required precedence over the old "A" goal. And some even get dropped off the list.)

Tactics:

1. Read about setting goals. See reference materials at end of the book.

2. Consistently keep your goals where you can read them.

3. If your goal is to obtain a tangible object—something you can see—have a picture of it and keep it where you can see it often. For example, when I started to write this book, I had a dummy cover created, covered an old book about the size I wanted this book to be, and laid it on the credenza in my office as a constant reminder.

4. Write short-term and long-term goals.

5. Be specific. Be very clear as to what you want. If you desire a small office, where will it be? What will it look like? How many people will work for you? Will it be simple or fancy? How soon do you plan to move in? How much will it cost? And so forth.

6. Don't be discouraged if you get off track or are falling behind your time schedule. That happens. Just re-evaluate that goal and decide how soon you need to get back on track.

7. *Do it!* You can read all the books in the world and listen to all the audio tapes, but unless you make yourself do it, you're wasting your time. Make a commitment today.

8. Write and monitor your goals using a system that works well for you; otherwise, you're setting yourself up for failure.

9. Share your goals with others—family, spouse, close friends—and ask for their support. You have to be a little creative with this tactic because occasionally your friends or family won't be supportive.

10. Share goals involving others who work with you so they can help you get there. Help them to see the big picture as you see it. Many times employers let their employees see only pieces of the puzzle and then wonder why the employees can't get excited or get things done correctly. Give them the entire puzzle.

11. When writing out your goals and plans to accomplish them, include obstacles you might encounter and how you will work around those obstacles.

The purpose of goals is to focus our attention. The mind will not reach toward achievement until it has clear objectives. The magic begins when we set goals. It is then that the switch is turned on, the current begins to flow, and the power to accomplish becomes reality.

Best of Success

What Does "Success" Mean to You?

Definitions of *success* are as varied as the people pursuing it. My definition of success—my definition of success for Joan Burge—may be very different from your definition of success for you and your business. You need to determine and specify what success is for you; if you haven't defined it, you won't know you've achieved it!

Success doesn't necessarily mean big house, fancy car, lots of money, and home in the Alps. I bet you have heard of many people who look successful on the outside but aren't really happy. When I say the word "success," I have my own vision of what success is. I expect your vision to be different. We shouldn't feel any less successful because we don't have a staff of fifty or our own corporate offices. I think if you are doing all you can and striving to be all you can become in this life, then you are successful. But you have to decide for yourself what success means.

Tactics:

1. **Define and measure your own success. Is success running a nice little business out of your home and making a**

moderate income or is it building a million-dollar corporation?

2. Refuse to allow anyone else to determine your success or make you feel less successful or like a failure. Decide for yourself if and when you are a success. When you feel good about who you are and the work you do, you'll know in your heart that you are a success and it won't matter what anyone else says.

3. Ignore others who measure your success by how much money you have or by the material things you own. To be truly successful, you feel contentment inside, you are at peace with others, and you are thankful for what you have.

4. Appreciate your position—the wonderful position of being an entrepreneur. Do you know how many people wake up every day, go to their mundane jobs, and never feel the exhilaration of creating a product or idea that benefits hundreds of people? There are thousands. So how is it you are so fortunate to be an entrepreneur?

> Commit your work to the Lord, then it will succeed.
>
> *Proverbs* 16:3

Learn From Every Experience

Experience—good or bad—is a great teacher. It's not always a gentle teacher, but it's a teacher nevertheless. You can learn from a bad experience. Some of my best lessons came from what most people would consider a negative experience. When you do something incorrectly or make a decision that wasn't necessarily the best decision, you will not forget it. And it won't happen again, if you learn to self-correct.

I learn every day. I meet new challenges, make new mistakes, am faced with new situations, and sometimes meet what I call "dragons," with whom I have to learn to deal. But every time I have an experience, especially a challenging one, I learn from it. I think about how I will handle this event should a similar one occur in the future or how I will adjust my thinking so I'll be prepared for the future.

It's kind of a cycle, however. You learn from an experience and plant it in your brain for the next time it happens. You get fairly adept at handling that particular situation or person in the future, but life keeps dealing you a new hand. It's a never-ending cycle.

Tactics:

1. Look for the lesson. There is *something* you should learn even if it's to never do that particular thing again.

2. Understand and appreciate that experience is better than any book or tape or seminar because you are the player. You can read all the available books, but until you go out and do it, implement what you read, make it a part of you, you really haven't learned the lesson.

3. When something has gone wrong, take time to reflect and evaluate what happened. Ask yourself questions similar to these:
   a. What went wrong?
   b. Was my thinking off?
   c. Did I use poor judgment?
   d. Did I do enough research?
   e. Did I really understand the issue?
   f. Did I get all the facts?
   g. What will I do should a similar situation occur in the future?
   h. What can I learn from this experience?

Don't be afraid to fail. Don't waste energy trying to cover up failure. Learn from your failures and go on to the next challenge. IT'S *OK* TO FAIL. If you're not failing, you're not growing.

H. Stanley Judd
Best of Success

Change Your Focus

When you have a problem, do you see a problem, or do you see a challenge? As an entrepreneur you are always going to have "problems." Personally, I don't use this word. Even in my most trying of moments, I say, "This is a real challenge."

If you look at a problem only as a problem, that is what you will tend to focus on—the problem. Such a focus tends to obscure possible solutions and make you think that your efforts will be fruitless. It gives the impression, a false one, that there might not *be* an answer.

In reality, there is always an answer to every problem. If you search long enough and possibly change your focus, you will find the solution. The solution, however, might not be the one you wanted and things might not turn out the way you anticipated; but even that outcome must be considered an answer.

When you are faced with your next problem, just imagine yourself saying "I have a real challenge ahead of me" or "This is an interesting opportunity." Those phrases alone leave an opening for feelings of success and achievement rather than giving you a feeling of defeat before you've even begun.

Tactics:

1. **Focus on the solution, not the problem.** Yes, you have to recognize and identify what the problem is but then put *all* your energies into finding the answer. This one small change will have a major impact on your ability to deal with the daily problems and major obstacles you will face.

2. Use the words *challenge* and *opportunity*. Start today. Eliminate the word *problem* from your vocabulary even in your personal life.

3. Encourage your employees to use the words *challenge* and *opportunity*.

4. Seek *creative* solutions.

5. Learn problem-solving techniques. There are several different methods to help you work through your challenges. Some are more structured methods and others more free-flowing, such as mind mapping or brainstorming.

6. Stop seeing that problem the way you've always seen it. Look at it in a different light. Search for what you *don't* see in black and white.

7. Ask for input or ideas from others. Sometimes we're too close to the situation. Sometimes we get tunnel vision and find that if we share a problem with other people they can instantly see what needs to be done or can offer a solution. This happened several times for me, but one incident that quickly comes to mind took place when I wrote my first book. I couldn't figure out the order of the chapters. I had twenty-one chapters written but no order of priority to them—which chapter should be first, second, and so on. A business associate whose judgment I trusted previewed the book and she easily saw how the chapters should progress. She saw a pattern of basic-to-advanced tactics. It was so simple for her, yet I had struggled with it for months.

8. See "no" as an answer and have the ability to accept it as an answer. Sometimes we're trying so hard to find the answer *we* want that we fail to see the answer as "not yet," "no," "it's not a good time for this idea," or "no, this idea just won't work."

9. Use a change of focus also to create new ideas for your business, increase productivity, and improve business systems. In other words, stop looking

at things the way you have always seen them or see them today. Start to ask "what if" questions. What if I try it this way? What if I change this? What if I make this smaller or larger? What if I train everyone to really understand the mission of this company and the integral role they play? What if I hire someone who is an expert in that area?

10. Consider the possibility that this challenge should be put on the back burner for awhile. (See Put It on the Back Burner.)

Each problem has hidden in it an opportunity so powerful that it literally dwarfs the problem. The greatest success stories were created by people who recognized a problem and turned it into an opportunity.

Joseph Sugarman
Best of Success

Make It Happen

Are you waiting for your partner to make things happen? Are you waiting for your sales reps to make things happen? Are you waiting for enough funds to make things happen? Are you waiting for more clients to make things happen?

Only *you* can make things happen in your business. Only you can motivate you in reality. Only you can get yourself to do what is necessary. Only you can make yourself a success. Yes, other things and events do come into play. Maybe the funds aren't available. Maybe your phone isn't ringing off the hook. Maybe your idea didn't work. But it is your choice as to how you handle those events.

Do you back off when you hit a roadblock or do you find a way around it? Do you beat yourself up mentally when you've made a mistake or poor decision or can you take that experience and turn it into a lesson? Do you sulk for days when things aren't going as you expected and everything you touch falls apart or do you bounce back quickly?

As a novice entrepreneur, you will hit many barriers and you can use the excuse that your dream just isn't meant to come true; or you can make adjustments, think of alternatives, and learn from those experiences.

Tactics:

1. Accept that *you* are responsible for making happen what you want in your business. If you want to have a business that grows year after year, that is up to you. You put the brakes on and only you can take the brakes off. And don't use the excuse that it's the economy that's stopping you. If things are tough, you'd better get out there and see more people, think more creatively, and maybe put in longer hours.

2. Believe that you can make your dreams come true once you identify the obstacles. Your belief system is vitally important. It will be critical to the success or failure of your business.

3. Write a plan and implement it. (See Chapter on Goal Mapping.)

4. Understand that negative answers and barriers are just tests as to how serious you really are about what you believe in. Tests as to how committed you are to your dream.

5. Be assertive. Go after what you want. In other words, don't sit around waiting for people to call you. Don't sit

around waiting for Lady Luck. Sometimes she doesn't show up.

6. Seek out business. Have plenty of
    things going on at once (but not so
    many that you can't do a good job
    with them). If you throw enough stuff
    out, eventually something is going to
    stick. If you have only one thing
    going for you and it's not working,
    you might get in trouble.

7. Learn to bounce back quickly after a
    setback. It is not the end of the world
    when you have a setback. It is *only* a
    setback. You must get on with life.
    Forge forward and keep faith. Keep
    believing and the answers will come.

8. Read inspirational materials and listen
    to motivational tapes when you feel
    your belief system wavering or when
    you believe that you can't take
    another day of rejection. We all have
    bad days. Bad weeks. I've even had
    bad months! And we all need to be
    uplifted during those times. Recognize
    what makes you feel good and seek
    out materials and people who lift you
    up.

The fulfillment of your dreams lies within you and you alone. When you understand and accept this, then nothing, or no one, can deny you greatness. The power to succeed or fail is yours. And no one can take that away.

The Best of Success

Change the Way You Look at Life

Do you see good or evil? Do you see what could go wrong or what could go right? Do you see a glass half-filled with water as half-empty or half-full? Do you see partly cloudy skies or partly sunny skies? The choice is yours. In other words, are you a pessimist or optimist?

The way you look at life can have a major impact on your decision-making process, impact on your use of your risk muscle, impact on your success as an entrepreneur. If you always look for what could go wrong and why something won't work, those things are what you will see. But if you look for what could go *right* and why something *will* work, then those things are what you will see.

I'm not advocating that you go around with rose-colored glasses all the time and not see the realities or dangers. What I am saying is that many people, many times, focus too much on the negative. And if that is where you focus, that is what you will see.

Tactics:

1. Understand that you can develop optimism. It's a habit. It might take time and you may slip several times but don't give up.

2. Practice optimism daily. Look for good outcomes. Look for the good in people. Look for at least one thing every day for which to be thankful.

3. Fill your mind with positive food/positive thoughts. The way to do that is to:
   — Have inspiring and profound quotes posted where you can see them daily. I have forty-one quotes typed on 8½ x 11 sheets of paper posted above my desk. With so many, I can select and focus on the one or two thoughts I need for that day or to help me get through a particularly difficult time.
   — Listen to audio tapes that are motivational.
   — Every morning, before you leave home, read an inspirational quote, a Psalm, or a spiritual message.
   — Go to sleep with a pleasant thought or read something pleasant just before sleeping.

4. **Catch yourself when you are having a negative thought.** *Stop it.* **And immediately get yourself focused on something positive.**

Become a possibilitarian. No matter how dark things seem to be or actually are, raise your sights and see the possibilities—always see them, for they're always there.

Norman Vincent Peale

Take a Break

I'll never forget a "free" presentation I gave on TQM at an association's monthly meeting. I was asked two weeks before their meeting to speak and feverishly did some research to add to the material I already had on the subject and prepared overheads and handouts.

Just prior to the invitation to speak at this event, I had been on a more-hectic-than-usual pace. For several weeks in a row I was conducting training daily, doing some guest speaking, attending evening business functions, and preparing to go out of town on business; my first book had just been released and I was happily busy with the publisher and media and was preparing for radio and newspaper interviews.

The night of my speech for this association, after spending forty-five minutes talking about the importance of quality work and service, explaining the importance of doing things right the first time, and the impact of employees doing things inefficiently, I was quite taken by surprise when one of the participants approached me after the program with my handout in hand and said "Were you testing us tonight?" I asked what he meant. With a big grin, he and another man questioned if I noticed the date on the cover of my handout. I probably looked bewildered as he showed me the cover which boldly had *April 20,*

19922! I'm sure you can imagine my embarrassment after forty-five minutes of preaching about doing things right the first time.

I had overextended myself with work to the point of being too tired to catch an error which strained my credibility. I knew I needed a break but, due to demands of the business, I didn't make time for myself. In retrospect, I never should have agreed to do that speech on that particular date. But I was new in the business and, of course, wanted the exposure. I sure got it, didn't I?

Tactics:

1. Don't allow your schedule to get so full that you don't have some time to replenish your mental and physical energy. Of course, it's hard to take a break when you are almost running your business yourself and trying to get it off the ground.

2. Make sure your secretary or assistant who helps in scheduling your appointments, if you have one, understands the importance of leaving you some time to catch your breath.

3. When you find your schedule is more than you really care to handle but must, find *some* opportunity to have quiet time. Create some small block of time for yourself.

4. Remember that when you get burned out you are not only hurting yourself, you're hurting your business. You will make mistakes, some of which could be costly. You may not do as good a job as you normally would, cause yourself embarrassment, lose credibility, and lose customers.

A man who refuses to admit his mistakes can never be successful

Proverbs 28:13

Act On It Now

It's so easy to procrastinate, isn't it? To hold off implementing an idea, making that sales call, committing yourself to writing that business plan. Why *do* people procrastinate? A few reasons are:

1. Fear holds them back. Fear of rejection. Fear an idea is stupid. Fear an idea won't work. And even fear of success.

2. The project is time-consuming and so one would rather keep putting it off than get it over with.

3. People get wrapped up in day-to-day business. The putting-out of fires, the responding to immediate decisions, phone calls, and meetings.

There are times we are forced to procrastinate because of our busy schedules, and sometimes we should purposely hold off on certain things such as making an important decision until all the facts are in or until we have contacted important resources. I'm not addressing that kind of procrastination. I'm talking about the times that you are afraid to do something and, therefore, you allow the fear to hold you back. Or the times you put something off just because it's something you're not looking forward to doing.

Sometimes we need to look at all that is lost by not acting on something today. As an entrepreneur, you really can't afford the luxury of procrastination. We live in a very competitive marketplace and what you might be thinking of today, someone else can have in the market tomorrow.

Tactics:

1. **Adjust your self-talk. Instead of telling yourself "I'll do this next week" or "This can wait until next month," train yourself to say "I'm going to do this now" and "I'm going to address that problem today" and "I'm going to implement that new idea today."**

2. **Remember that tomorrow may be too late.**

3. **Muster up the tremendous amount of discipline that it takes to get in the habit of not procrastinating. If you can discipline yourself to not procrastinate, you will speed up your success record. Discipline yourself to do it *now*.**

4. **Walk your talk. Don't just talk about what you'd like to do or get others excited about an idea and then drop**

it. If you believe in something, if you believe your idea has value and you want to do it, then *do* it. Show people and yourself all the good stuff you're really made of. So many people in our society are good at talking about what they think should be done or talking about what others should do and how they would do it differently or better if they were in a similar situation. To be a successful entrepreneur, one of the qualities you must possess is the characteristic of being a *person of action*.

Our expectancies not only affect how we see reality, but also affect reality itself.

Edward E. Jones

Cycle of Achievement

Do things, even little things that will allow you success and thus give you a sense of achievement. When you have a sense of achievement, you will feel good and will be encouraged to do more, to take further action.

If you hit a roadblock or you take action on something that totally blows up in your face, put it behind you and move forward. Go to the next action. I hear people say that they attempted something or many things which failed and so they are too discouraged to try again. Don't give up. Eventually you will achieve. It might be that you just haven't hit upon the right thing. It could also be that you're having tunnel vision and not opening up your eyes to opportunities that could lead to success. It could be that you gave up too easily, or that you are trying too hard to make something work, or 101 other reasons.

Tactics:

1. Select work that ties in with your strengths, abilities, and talents.

2. Take little steps to achievement. In other words, select a small challenge, something that will cause you to stretch just a little but that could turn out successful for you. Once you accomplish that, take on a little bigger challenge or something equally challenging.

3. Notice when you succeed. Give yourself a pat on the back. Tell yourself you did a good job.

4. Don't get discouraged when you don't achieve. Go on to something else.

5. Sit down once in a while and make a list of all the things you have accomplished. A good time to do this is after about one year of being in business. The time goes quickly the first year and usually you are so buried in your work that you don't take time to step back and look at the progress you have made. So at the end of about a year, write out all the things you did. Don't forget the little things. They all add up.

For the man who uses well what he is given shall be given more, and he shall have abundance.

Matthew 25:29

Personal Growing Pains

Part of the old Joan Burge had to die so that a different, better Joan Burge could emerge. For twenty years I worked for other companies, always had a boss, received a regular paycheck, and, most of the time, had job security. I then became Joan Burge, founder and president of Office Dynamics. Joan Burge. . .national speaker, trainer and eventually author. How does one change overnight? Employee one day, entrepreneur the next. Not easily.

Your title might change, and your position as an entrepreneur might be new. But the *you* inside doesn't change that easily or that quickly. It takes time and can sometimes be painful.

Tactics:

1. Shed some of those old layers of you that have built up over the years. Shed the ones that are of no use now or could be holding you back from becoming all you are capable of becoming. It may be a painful process but after a while you will look back as I did and realize that the pain is gone and you will be happy you made the change.

2. Be patient as you labor through the birth of a new you. You might be tempted to jump back to that old comfortable you, but don't do it.

3. Understand that as you grow and change, you may start to look differently at friends and family. You may find that you have outgrown some of your old friendships. You will replace some of them with new friendships. Friends and peers that are maybe more in line with your thinking now, people with whom you can grow and from whom you can learn, and whom you can nurture.

4. See the new you mentally—see yourself in your new role, acting and speaking in that new role.

5. Keep some of the old you, too. Hang tight to your old good qualities. Don't forget to stop, have fun, and enjoy family and friends.

> Next to being what we ought to be, the most desirable thing is that we should become what we ought to be as fast as possible.
>
> Herbert Spencer

Create a Niche

You can capitalize on opportunity by creating a niche. For example, in my business of training, speaking, and consulting, there are thousands of trainers and consultants in the world. But at the onset of my business, I decided to concentrate on developing training for administrative staff and middle management. I knew from working for twenty years in a variety of business environments that administrative staff are integral players in an organization and yet are the least trained and most neglected.

Then, within that niche, I went another step and designed a unique training series for just that workforce segment. I came up with a concept that grew like a web into several other areas. Next I focused on developing a trademark for myself and the business. Actually, as so often happens, it didn't start out that way but it quickly evolved and, after twelve months, I intentionally started to play off my company logo and trademark of a "star." Let me tell you how this grew and then maybe you can apply this concept to your business or service.

When Office Dynamics was started, a logo was designed. It was a contemporary star with the company name Office Dynamics across the star. The first published article I wrote was called "Star Performance. . .Do You Have What It

Takes?" The first training series I wrote was called the Star Achievement™ Series. Then I wrote an Advanced Star Achievement™ Series. While all this was going on, I used stars as rewards to participants at my seminars, handed them out when appearing for guest speaking engagements, used stars at my display tables when exhibiting, started getting gift items with stars, and began to wear accessories with stars. I started an organization called the Star Achievers® and most recently published my first audio cassette program called "Star Performance."

When I'm out attending professional organizational meetings or conventions, it is not at all unusual for people to come up to me and say "I know you, Joan. You're the lady with the stars."

Tactics:

1. Within your industry or field, think of how you can build a niche. How can you develop a twist to what everyone else is doing?

2. Think of how you can do it better—more creatively—with a more contemporary twist—for today's world.

3. Develop a theme and carry it through in everything you do or create. Eventually, you will become known for that particular thing. People will remember you. And if they remember

you, they will remember your product or service.

4. Don't be afraid to be unique. To use something people can connect to you. I met a speaker in the summer of 1992 who calls herself a propeller. She has a propeller on everything from her stationery to newsletters to envelopes.

To be a star, you must shine your own light, follow your path, and don't worry about the darkness, for that is when stars shine brightest.

Maximize Your Peak Time of Day

Are you an early-morning person? Late-morning person? Afternoon person? In other words, when are you at your best? When are you really mentally alert and physically energetic?

The morning is my very best time of day, the time when I get the most accomplished. That is when my most creative moments occur and when my thinking is most clear. So I use that time of day to:

— Make major decisions,
— Work on major projects, creative ideas, or tasks I don't like to perform,
— Write speeches, training programs, and educational articles and books,
— Visit that difficult client,
— Give that challenging presentation,
— Make that tough sales call.

Tactics:

1. Identify your peak time of day.

2. Plan to do those tasks that require the best of you during your peak time, if at all possible.

3. Use your low-energy time of day to do mundane tasks, make routine phone calls, organize your work, pay bills, and meet with people who don't require a lot of energy from you.

4. During your peak period, whenever possible, keep away distractions. Or ask those around you to keep others away. You will get so much more accomplished.

5. Stay focused. When working during your peak time, you must keep yourself focused to fully utilize this time. Don't jump from one thing to another; be wary of starting a writing project, stopping to pick up the phone to make a call, jumping back to your project, then making another call, then jumping over to something else. Staying focused is not easy for everyone because some people are more easily distracted while others can spend a great deal of time on internal reflection. If you find yourself jumping around in this fashion, concentrate on resisting the temptation.

> We learn things consciously,
> but we will never do them well
> until we learn to do them subconsciously.

Put It On the Back Burner

When you are working on solutions to challenges and opportunities or trying to come up with a unique way to promote your product or write that enticing newspaper ad, there will be times that you have a mental block. When you just don't have any creative ideas flowing. A time when no thoughts come to your mind about what you are working on. What can you do? You can sit, fret, and try to make yourself come up with ideas, but this approach doesn't always work well. Sometimes it is better to put it on the back burner.

When you put it on the back burner, or just put the project aside, you have really buried it into your subconscious. And then at some time, when you least expect it, the answer will come to mind—at 2:00 a.m., while you're driving, when you're in church or in the shower.

This happens to me frequently. I do a tremendous amount of creating and writing, designing exciting and educational training programs, books, educational articles, coming up with ideas for my organization, and more. Quite often I get a mental block about a project and can go for only so long, maybe a couple of hours, before the thoughts stop flowing. I just put it aside and, before I know it, later the thoughts come freely and creatively.

Tactics:

1. Remember that being an entrepreneur is exciting because you have freedom to use as much creativity as your heart desires, but it also means that there are times when you will have no answers.

2. Don't panic. When your mind is blank or you can't figure something out, remember that your answers will eventually come if you continue to have a seeking mind and keep your mind open. Many times the things, people, and places around you will have a connection to what you are working on. So commit to keeping your ears open, your mind open, and your eyes open.

3. Keep a tape recorder in your car. It's amazing how many things you think of when driving. Why not capture those thoughts immediately? You rarely remember those brilliant thoughts exactly as you first had them, and sometimes you don't remember them at all. Or how many of you try to write your idea while you're driving? Not easy, right? I carry a little tape recorder in my car and leave it on the seat next to me. Every time I get a thought I want to remember, I talk

into the recorder. Then after a few days, unless critical information on the tape makes me retrieve it sooner, I take it out and play back my ideas. Sometimes I'm amazed at some of the things I said or ideas I had on the tape that I forgot I dictated. I'm always glad I captured them on tape.

The only limit to our realization of tomorrow will be our doubts of today.

Franklin D. Roosevelt
Best of Success

Shut Yourself Down

It was fifteen months after I started my business when I first permitted myself to not think about Office Dynamics for five days in a row. It was Christmas holiday 1991; my husband, our children, and I went to spend the holiday with my family. After five great days of laughter and relaxation, my husband said to me, "You haven't mentioned your business once since we've been here." I didn't realize until that moment that I hadn't had business on my mind once in five days.

I returned home so refreshed and energized that I got more accomplished in one week than I normally would have over a period of several weeks. My thoughts were clear, my creative level was high, and I felt unstoppable. I had renewed enthusiasm and was able to make decisions on some projects I had put on hold.

Tactics:

1. Force yourself to take a break. When you are an entrepreneur and you love what you do, it's easy to just keep going. You just keep going and going.

2. Recognize that one of the hazards of being a one-man team is that you feel more obligated to not take a break. You can develop a thought process which says "I can't take a break. I have to keep working. I have a business to grow." The truth is that you *have* to take break. I don't mean one day here and a weekend now and then. I mean a real break. A break where you don't just physically get away, but you are *mentally* away from the business.

3. Get out of focus so you can get better focus. Purposely change your focus to fun, to relaxation, to friends. Then, when you get back to work, you will have more focus than before. You will keep focused on work and what you need to do; without such a break you will find yourself focusing on the fact that you never have free time any more, see your friends, or go out and enjoy the sunshine.

4. Don't feel guilty. You are entitled to a break. You're entitled to enjoy all aspects of life.

> Go as far as you can see,
> and when you get there,
> you will always be able to see further.

Enjoy the Process

As entrepreneurs, especially in those first few years, we're anxious for time to pass so we can see and experience the success we dream of having. We also spend a great deal of time planning and thinking *future*. Thinking about the next hurdle we need to overcome. Then, of course, once we overcome one hurdle, we set another hurdle to overcome.

The process itself—the process of getting there—should be just as rewarding. And for many people, it's the process they love more than actually reaching the goal. If you don't enjoy every day of climbing that mountain, when you finally reach it you might feel terribly empty and unsatisfied.

Tactics:

1. **Enjoy every day of your life. Make sure that you enjoy the good things that happen as well as appreciate the tough challenges.**

2. **Think how fortunate you are to be an entrepreneur—a great expression of personal freedom. What a wonderful thing to be doing what you love.**

Entrepreneurs are doing what they love or have a talent for; otherwise they would be working for someone else.

3. Force yourself to stop and appreciate today. It's easy to get busy and excited about your work and where it's heading, especially if you're on a roll. So, stop and enjoy.

4. Take time to reflect on your accomplishments. Two things I have maintained since the day I started my business are a scrap book and a personal diary. Every so often I pull out my scrap book, which is filled with photos of my first office, my first secretary, my stationery, copies of advertisements, thank-you letters from clients, flyers from seminars I've conducted, and newspaper articles. I look through that—two books, now—and realize how far I really have come in 2½ years. These glances back are especially helpful when maybe I am feeling impatient with my progress. My computer diary is a reminder of the tough times, the sleepless nights, and the wonderful moments. I use it, too, as a reminder of why I'm doing what I'm doing and to remind me of the hardships I thought I would never overcome and did.

Think enthusiastically about everything; but especially about your job. If you do, you'll put a touch of glory in your life. If you love your job with enthusiasm, you'll shake it to pieces. You'll love it into greatness, you'll upgrade it, you'll fill it with prestige and power.

Norman Vincent Peale

Network

Network. You hear this word all the time. In fact, you might be sick of hearing it. The fact is, there is networking, and then there is *networking.* And everyone who thinks he's doing it may not really be doing it.

Networking is getting to know others. Getting to know what they do, their talents, and their interests and seeing how they can fit in or help you reach your goal and how you can help them. Networking is different than supporting. My definition of supporting, in a business sense, is being available to others and providing encouragement. Support is "being there" for someone with no ulterior motives and without expectations of getting anything in return.

Networking is a valuable skill to novice entrepreneurs as well as master entrepreneurs. You never know how or when the person you meet today and with whom you build a relationship can help you in the future. Networking can benefit you in many ways. Here are just a few:

— It can help you gain untapped knowledge.
— It can be used to let others know your strengths and talents so they can help promote you.
— It can make you aware of many other resources that you didn't even know existed and that could help you in what you

are doing. I've experienced this benefit several times.

Tactics:

1. **Don't underestimate the value of networking.**

2. **Consistently practice the skill of true networking.**

3. **Be aware that networking takes having an open mind to all people and training your mind to seek out your connection with others—who they are, what they do, and who they know.**

4. **Keep networking constructive; it should not be manipulative.**

5. **Build networks and develop your networking skills through committee work, community work, church, business functions, seminars, client/customer relations, vendors, charity work, and your children's activities. And don't forget friends and family.**

> Do for others what you want them to do for you.
>
> *Matthew* 7:12

Stretch, Stretch, and Then Stretch Again

Most people love to stay in their comfort zones. They continue to do things that are safe and comfortable, continue to "hang out" with people that make them comfortable rather than encourage growth. This tendency is the quickest path to personal and mental death for an entrepreneur. Entrepreneurs cannot work in comfort zones and expect their businesses to grow or expect to be personally successful.

Success, as we have seen, is different for all of us, and there are various degrees of success. But to achieve growth, you must stretch. I constantly stretched in starting my business and I still stretch. It is my plan to continue stretching—to continue challenging myself and my talents and dealing with my fears.

When you stretch, you grow. And growth is good. I know if you have the spirit of a true entrepreneur, you will apply this consistently.

STRETCHING = GROWTH

Tactics:

1. **Force yourself to stretch.** Initially and periodically, you may have to force

yourself out of your comfort zones. Make yourself do something that will cause you to stretch and that will help you grow.

2. Stretch again. Once you've stretched out of your comfort zone, do it again and again, each time taking on a little bigger challenge. You don't have to stretch immediately one time after another, day after day, month after month. Just do one thing that makes you stretch and then maybe a few months or six months later take on something else that causes you to stretch.

3. Understand that stretching equals growth. This is such an easy concept, but few people apply it. Think of something in your life that initially was difficult—uncomfortable—but you stuck it out and eventually it became comfortable for you. You can't be growing if you are standing still, if you are stagnant. It just is not possible to stretch and stand still at the same time.

4. Be creative. Think of things you can do or projects related to your business you can create to make yourself stretch.

5. Remember that your rewards will be many. You might very well experience a feeling of exhilaration after you stretch and see the benefits of that stretch.

6. Whenever life presents you with a challenge, go forward rather than backing off. If you need to learn a certain skill, then learn it. But don't get scared and back off.

7. Reward yourself or at least take a moment to mentally compliment yourself. Reinforce the fact that you stepped out of your comfort area, survived, and maybe even excelled.

The greatest trouble with most of us is that our demands upon ourselves are so feeble, the call upon the great within us so weak and intermittent that it makes no impression upon the creative energies: it lacks force that transmutes desires into realities.

Osison Swett Marden

Win-Win Situations

As entrepreneurs and business creators we have to look for opportunities to help others which will also help us and our businesses. I've been fortunate in developing what I call win-win situations, many of which, with continuous nurturing, turned into long-term business relationships for me.

You can't make it in this world alone, and you can't make it as an entrepreneur alone. We all need each other. The beauty is that when we support others and they support us, everyone wins. And, little by little, your network grows. You will have more people helping you and spreading the word about you and your services or products.

Tactics:

1. **Whenever you meet someone, get to know him/her and see if there is any way the two of you connect. What do you have in common with this person? Are you both trying to reach the same customer yet you're not competitors?**

2. Make sure that both of you win, not just you and your company.

3. Consider someone's knowledge as an offering. It doesn't always have to be a tangible item you gain. The gift of knowledge and expertise can be just as valuable as, sometimes even more valuable than, any tangible item you could receive.

4. You might do some bartering that will help with your expenses and benefit you in other ways.

5. Make a habit of looking for win-win situations. Team up with other people who can help you and to whom you have something to offer.

6. Remember that others can see opportunities you may not see because you're too close to a situation.

7. The benefits of creating win-win situations are many:
   a. Great way to cut expenses.
   b. That person might have knowledge to offer.
   c. More people to do the labor.
   d. Increased creativity.
   e. Increased exposure for both parties.

8. Every time you make a contact, think to yourself, "Does this person have

something I want? Can this person help me get more exposure? Can this person's business use my services or products or use my service as a gift to their customers?" In other words, what, if any, is the link between you and this person, your goals and his goals?

9. Make sure both parties win. It's not good if only one of you wins or one feels the other is not doing his share.

10. Don't misconstrue networking to mean "use other people." I definitely am not implying that you use others.

> Change starts when someone sees the next step.
>
> William Drayton

Challenges of a Service Business

How do you sell something that is intangible? How do you get people to buy something they can't touch, feel or see? Or measure its value? You can do it, as I have, but it's not easy.

Selling a service, such as a consulting business or an answering service, is more challenging than selling a product such as computers, clothing, art work, and other tangibles. It's especially challenging when your business is new and you don't have clients you can use as referrals.

Tactics:

1. Sell the *benefits* of your service. Understanding this concept took me a while. At first I was selling my training programs. I was selling Joan Burge. I started to realize, with the help of professional sales people and my husband, that I'm selling benefits. My clients and their staff benefit from my training. They benefit in many ways, and *that's* what I needed to show them.

2. Once you establish satisfied clients,
   a. Get testimonials from them in writing that you can share with potential customers;
   b. Ask if they would mind potential clients calling them for a recommendation;
   c. Ask them for names and phone numbers of others who might benefit from your service.

3. Learn how to sell. I knew how to train, meet people, write, and organize my business. What I didn't know was how to sell. So with the help of my husband, who has been in sales for years, and some good books, I learned about selling. I'm still learning but I know I have changed my thoughts about selling and have learned some valuable techniques.

4. After you get yourself up and running, think about whether there is any way you can turn your service into tangible products as an extension of the service. For example, if you have a cleaning service or maid service, you might put together a little booklet on how to maintain your home or how to care for special appliances, wood floors, or fabrics that you could sell to your customers. They can use this

guide to help maintain their home in between the times your people go to clean.

If we want to change a situation, we must first change ourselves And to change ourselves effectively, we must first change our perceptions.

Stephen R. Covey

The At-Home Office

The home office is becoming very popular in this decade. There are several reasons for its popularity. There is a surge of entrepreneurs today, and many of them are starting their businesses from their homes. Some companies, in trying to meet the needs of their employees as well as cut expenses, are allowing and encouraging employees to work in their homes or use their homes as a base. In some instances, a home office is used in addition to the out-of-home office. Finally, many working mothers are seeking businesses that allow them to be at home so they can be with their children.

Each entrepreneur has to weigh the value and reality of having an at-home office. It's a great place to start and maintain a business until you are bringing in enough income to justify having an out-of-home office. On the other hand, you may never need an out-of-home office. Much depends on what you do and how much you want to grow.

Tactics:

1. Keep regular working hours, whether they are 8:00-5:00 or 7:30-4:30 or 7:00-

4:00. Keep a schedule as if you had to go to an office outside your home.

2. Let your children and other family members know the rules. One rule might be that you're not to be disturbed except for emergencies. Or that you have set times of the day you will try to take breaks, such as when the children come home from school.

3. Caution: You do have to watch that you don't often overextend office hours. It's too easy to go in the office in the evening and on weekends. Many times, as a novice entrepreneur, you need to. But you also can overdo. (See Take A Break.)

4. Keep your at-home office looking like an office. It is an office. View it as a place of business. Don't have cutesy things displayed all around or have laundry sitting in a basket. If your office visually is a "real" office, you will be more inclined to be in a business frame of mind.

5. If you are a woman who normally wears make-up, you should put it on every day. It will make you feel good, and that feeling comes across when you deal with people on the telephone.

6. Have a separate phone line installed and make it perfectly clear that no one else in the house answers that phone. Use a separate telephone answering service to handle your calls. I find this especially beneficial because 1) someone is always there to take your calls, 2) if you have a good service, many times people think they are really reaching your office instead of a service, 3) potential customers won't be discouraged by a busy signal or distracted by call-waiting, and 4) with some services, you can select your own phone number.

7. Don't get side-tracked and do household chores or be tempted to turn on the TV. Just imagine that you are at an office outside your home. Would you be doing household chores?

8. Invest in a good computer system and comfortable, practical office furniture. Don't try to use a folding table and grab the kitchen chair. I'm not saying you have to invest a lot of money, but set yourself up functionally.

9. Decide when it's time to move out. There are many advantages in working in your home, but for many busi-

nesses there may come a day when you need to push yourself out—expand.

> Where you go from here is entirely up to you.

Media

What an opportunity. The first page of the Business Section of Cleveland's major newspaper—a picture of me—the biggest one ever in the paper—dead center—Saturday paper. Sounds like a dream come true, doesn't it? Unfortunately, not necessarily. Not when what you say in a face-to-face interview is then left in the hands of a newspaper editor who misconstrues what you say and slants the story of the article to meet her needs. Media opportunities do not always meet your expectations.

When my first book was published, I was fortunate to get some publicity in a few newspapers as well as appearances on radio and TV, 95 percent of which was excellent and accurately represented my book.

However, that small amount of off-the-mark publicity—that 5 percent which inaccurately represents your efforts—can, if you allow it to, put a damper on your otherwise high spirits. Regarding my experience with the Cleveland paper, the Publicity Director at my publisher's office said, "At least you were in the paper." Interestingly, several people who read that article thought it was great. In fact, that afternoon I was doing book signings at two different stores and some people who purchased my book said they knew who I was. They remembered seeing my picture in the morning paper. Maybe I just had different expectations of what story would get printed.

Tactics:

1. Get educated about how to work with media people. There are good books which I obviously hadn't read until after my first disappointing experience with the media. I encourage you to read them if there is any possibility that you might be interviewed.

2. If an interview isn't going where you want it to, change direction. Don't feel intimated by these people or feel you have no control. I learned this the hard way.

3. Build a rapport with the person doing the interview. Try to establish a comfortable relationship.

4. Sometimes you can contribute the article yourself. I did that for a trade newsletter and even got paid.

When you're talking to the media, be a well, not a fountain.

Michael Deaver

Invest in Yourself

What do you think is your most valuable asset? Your building? Your staff? Your product? Your equipment? If you answered any of these or had a similar answer, your answer is incorrect. Yes, I said *incorrect*.

Your most valuable, precious, important asset of your business is *you*. The other things and people are important and necessary and shouldn't be overlooked. But without you, without your vision, without your knowledge, without your lifeblood, your business wouldn't even be born. There is only *one* of you.

And so you must learn to nurture yourself. Nurture your mind with knowledge. We are in an extremely competitive marketplace. The pace of change is accelerating. The only way to keep up with it all is by investing in knowledge. I can't stress enough the importance of becoming a life-long student. I'm not saying you better hurry up, run down to your local college, and sign up for life! I am saying you need to feed your brain just as you feed your body.

How do you decide what to buy? The possibilities seem endless. My husband and I have collected more than 275 books, eighteen audio cassette albums, and sixty single audio cassettes in just the past four years. This doesn't include the newspapers, periodicals, trade magazines, and professional organization newsletters I read. The topics vary. Today, one has to have knowledge in all aspects of business and life. For a novice entrepreneur there are some specific books I recommend, some of which are listed at the end of this book. It is also helpful to browse in the Small Business section of book stores. You will find many books to choose from. Maybe that's where you got this one.

Tactics:

1. Use the tools available for your continued education. The following are just a few: books, trade journals, business periodicals, audio cassettes and video tapes, seminars, conventions, professional organizations, peers, and mentors.

2. See the cost of these tools as an *investment*, not an *expense*. Don't say to yourself "I can't afford to do that right now" or "I've got to invest all my money in buying things for my business." Every time you invest in a book, in a seminar, in an audio tape, you are investing in you. When you invest in yourself, your investment remains with you always. No one can take it away, and you can always take that knowledge with you no matter where you go in life.

3. If you listen to audio cassettes, you should listen to them at least four to six times in order for everything to sink in. If you listen to tapes while you're driving, which is my favorite time, you will occasionally get distracted and find that you don't really hear parts of the message. Also, it's hard to absorb and fully concentrate on a great deal of material at once. I have many tapes I listen to over and over, put away for awhile, and then pull out again four to six months later. They are great refreshers!

4. In addition to knowledge, there are two other areas that are important for you to invest in: your health and your spiritual life. If you aren't healthy and you are the one running the business, there won't be a business. So take time to stay healthy. Make time also for spiritual readings. They are extremely uplifting, especially during those times when you might feel discouraged, hopeless, and having a just-plain-old tough time.

> Receive my *instruction,* and not silver; and *knowledge* rather than choice gold. For wisdom *is* better than rubies; and all things that may be desired are not to be compared to it.
>
> *Proverbs* 8:10-11

A Final Word

Mr. or Ms. Entrepreneur, whoever you are, wherever you are, I wish you the very best of luck. My first year was really tough and the second year was almost as tough. And my third year so far has presented me with many new challenges. It isn't an easy road, but I wouldn't trade any of it for a cushy job behind a desk working for someone else.

As I look back to almost three years ago (it will be three years for me at the time of the release of this book), I can't believe how fast time has gone and how much I have grown. Some may say I'm presumptuous offering advice after only three years as an entrepreneur; but the very freshness of my memories of being a novice entrepreneur is what makes my advice have merit (besides—it shouldn't matter to as how long I've been in business as much as what I accomplished in that time and what lessons I learned). I hope my book prepares you a little bit more than I was prepared because no one told me about many of the things I've shared with you. I learned many of them the hard way. Your road may not be an easy one either. But if you can follow some of the advice in my book—most importantly, remember Patience, Persistence, Faith, and Commitment—I think you'll be O.K. I hope three years from now you can look back and be satisfied with your decision to be an entrepreneur.

Good luck and God bless!

Reference Materials

Guerilla Marketing by Jay Conrad Levinson (Houghton & Mifflin).

Professional Speaking by Lilyan Wilder & John Naisbitt (Simon & Schuster).

Charting Your Goals by Dan Dahl & Randolph Sykes (Harper & Row).

The Deming Route to Quality and Productivity by W.W. Scherkenbach (Ceep Press Books).

Thriving on Chaos by Tom Peters (Knopf).

Quality is Free by Philip B. Crosby (McGraw Hill Book Company).

Wishcraft by Barbara Sher (Ballantine).

Save Your Business by Dick Parise (Hampton Roads Publishing Co.).

The Entrepreneur & Small Business Problem Solver by William A. Cohen (John Wiley & Sons).

Risk to Win by Jeannette R. Scollard (MacMillan).

The One Minute Sales Person by Spencer Johnson, M.D., & Larry Wilson (Morrow).

Unlimited Power by Anthony Robbins (Fawcett Columbine).

The Instant Millionaire by Mark Fisher (New World Library).

Negotiating to Close by Gary Karrass (Simon & Schuster).

Never Be Nervous Again by Dorothy Sarnoff (Crown).

The Power of Persuasion by G. Ray Funkhouser, Ph.D. (Times).

How to Master the Art of Selling by Tom Hopkins (Tom Hopkins International).

Swim With the Sharks by Harvey Mackay (Morrow).

Even Eagles Need a Push by David McNally (Transform Press).

Life Application Bible (Lyndale House).

The Best of Success (Celebrating Excellence, 919 Springer Drive, Lombard, IL 60148-6416, 708-953-8440).

Any of Og Mandino's books, especially:
Mission Success
Return of the Ragpicker
A Better Way to Live
The University of Success
The Choice
The Greatest Salesman in the World

Any audio and video tapes by Brian Tracy.

There is a vast selection of books in the Small Business Section of libraries relative to writing a business plan, finding venture capital, how to incorporate, hiring and interviewing, exporting, franchising and more.

About The Author

As a consultant, trainer, speaker and author specializing in the area of Star Achievement™, Joan M. Burge is uniquely qualified to offer insight into the challenges a Novice Entrepreneur faces in today's marketplace.

After twenty years of working as an executive assistant for twelve different companies ranging in size from small businesses to Fortune 500 companies, Joan Burge went on to become President and founder of Office Dynamics. She grew into a dynamic speaker, trainer, consultant, and author specializing in Star Achievement. In just two and half short years, she wrote her first book, *The Survival Guide for Secretaries and Administrative Assistants*, started her own professional organization, was conducting training for major corporations, published her first audio cassette program, and wrote numerous educational articles in addition to filling her roles as wife and mother of two children.

Now a much sought-after national speaker and trainer to major corporations, universities, numerous government agencies and small businesses, Joan shares with you the secrets of what helped her get through those first rough years as an entrepreneur.